MW01446348

We're taught we have to watch what we say when little ears are present, but good news; there is a loophole. Even though society and dirty minds have taken away so many expressions, the innocence of children allows us to bring them back and get some cheap chuckles along the way.

Take a moment to relax, unwind and enjoy the moments that follow.

Sunshine

enjoy the journey!
Sunshine

BLUE BALLS

Parenting is dirty business

created by Sunshine Sweet

illustrated by Emmi Ojala

copyright © 2014 Potty Talk, LLC
ISBN 978-0-9907852-0-0

www.blueballsbook.com

Giving a "helping hand"

I DON'T SWALLOW.

LICK FROM THE BOTTOM UP.

DON'T RUB HER KITTY SO HARD.

DON'T CHOKE THE CHICKEN!

ONLY MOMMY AND DADDY CAN SCREW.

LET ME GET YOUR ZIPPER.

LET'S GO FOR A QUICKIE.

Playing around

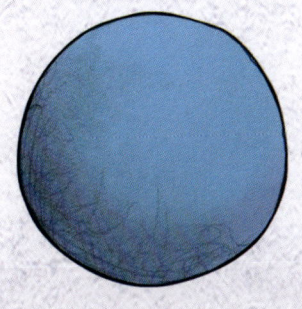

I GO BOTH ways.

DON'T STOP! DON'T STOP!

WHAT IS YOUR FAVORITE POSITION?

IT'S BETTER ON TOP.

IS THIS YOUR FIRST TIME?

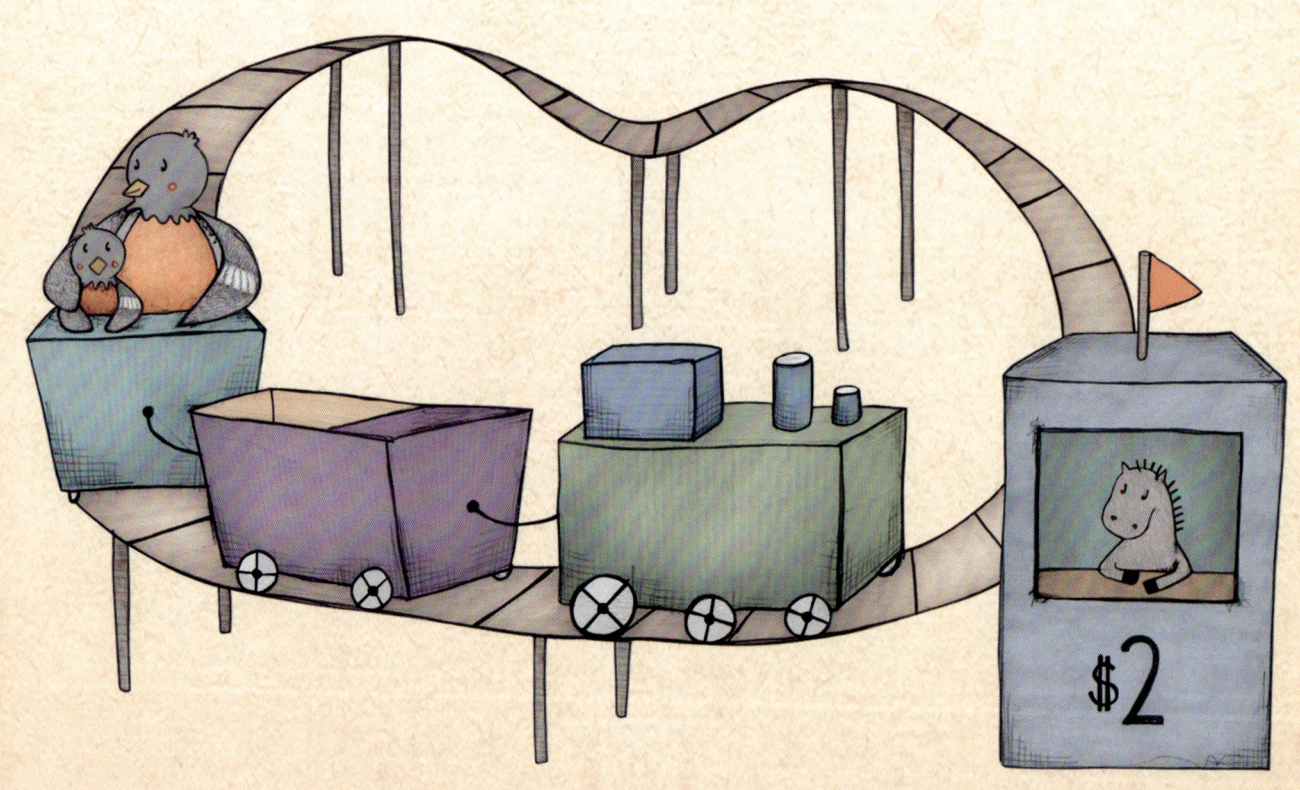

PUT IT IN
SLOWLY.

RUB ONE OUT.

LET'S DO A THREESOME!

YOUR PACKAGE IS **HUGE**!

I WANT A BOYTOY.

LET HIM GET OFF BY HIMSELF.

TAKE MY CHERRY.